Melt The Ice

Melt The Ice

By Marsha D. Stonehill

First Printing: 2020

ISBN: 9798636247722

Book Images and Cover Design belong to Marsha D. Stonehill
by E.R. – Hand drawn by Emily M. Rodes

Ordering Information:

Special discounts are available on quantity purchases by corporations, associations, educators, and others. For details, contact the publisher with the information below.

U.S. trade bookstores and wholesalers: Please contact the author:
melttheicellc@gmail.com

Contents

Acknowledgments

There are so many people who touched my life and inspired me to write this book. Each of these people contributed to my journey and personal growth, and there are too many to name individually.

My deepest thanks to the people in my life who confided in, supported, challenged, and believed in me.

–Marsha D. Stonehill, MSN, PMHNP/CNS, BC

Special Acknowledgements

Special thanks to the following 3 women:

Special Gratitude to Mrs. Julie C. Chatman,
MBA @ JulieChatman@gmail.com

My utmost gratitude to Mrs. Chatman who
took my original manuscript which was a
very disorganized thought storm filled with
clinical language. She courageously traveled
into this material, had conversations with
me, grasped the vision, and transformed it
into material that was more inviting and
carried a better flow for the reader. Without
her skilled labor into this manuscript,
publishing would not have been possible.
Thank you Mrs.Chatman for caring about
the material enough to dive into such a
mess. Yet another beautiful learning
experience for me.

To the Illustrator: Emily M. Rodes

Thank you for the time you spent delving into
this material and for listening so intently. You
successfully captured the simplicity I was
seeking and that was on one try! I anticipate that
the illustrations you created will speak volumes

in ways that more words cannot. The expansiveness of your artistic talents are quite a gift. Thank you for sharing your gift with me.

And, to the woman who wishes to remain anonymous:

Thank you for your creation of the graphic images tailored for this book and *Melt The Ice*. Thank you for helping extensively to tie up all the loose ends, create a final format and help me to take the leap of self-publishing. Thank you for your time, talents, encouragement, and feedback that brought it all together!

Power and Strength in Unexpected Places

"...we are also being reminded that we are all on a long journey of the soul. On this journey we encounter endless turns, shifts, and conditions that cause us to morph into ever–finer beings. At our soul–journeys end, we are inevitably changed and not at all the same as when we started on the path."

Those words are from https://www.spirit-animals.com/butterfly-symbolism/– a website I visited shortly after sitting with my 12–year–old German Shepherd as she transitioned to the other side. Butterfly wings represent transformation, tranquility, and confidence. Whenever I see a butterfly, I am reminded of the importance of embracing transitions.

Each of us can learn how to respond to life from the power that dwells inside us rather than falling into the conditioning this body and existence creates. May we all allow our wings to help us soar despite the hardships we encounter. This is our opportunity. This is our lesson.

What this Book Is and What It's Not

This book is a resource...

- For those who are inclined to be sensitive in a world that doesn't seem to recognize the value of sensitivity.
- To help people reconnect with the part of themselves that guides them towards fulfillment.
- That offers new opportunities for self–discovery by inviting readers to step outside their comfort zones and into the fullness of their strengths.

You can use the material in this book to...

- Increase self–awareness and facilitate personal growth.
- Develop a deeper understanding of and connection with people in your life.
- Understand how interconnectedness impacts your perceptions and interactions.
- Reinforce what you've already achieved and complement what you're currently working

on with your healthcare provider, therapist, or support group.

This book is not "psychobabble". It is a tool to help you explore ways to achieve greater happiness, peace, confidence, and self–control.

Important: This book is not a substitute for individualized professional guidance from a mental health professional or other healthcare provider. If you're currently under the supervision of a healthcare provider, continue to consult with them for instructions and support.

No material contained in this book disputes the existence of mental illness or the utility of medications designed to treat mental illness. Readers who are using medications should not stop taking those medications without instructions from their healthcare provider.

If you are in distress and not under the supervision of a healthcare provider, please seek help immediately.

Image and Figures

The figures and images in this book are tools to open up aspects of ourselves in ways that words cannot accomplish. Take time to look at the images and allow them to resonate with you according to your personal needs and experiences.

Introduction

My name is Marsha Stonehill and I'm a healer at heart and by trade. I've been a Registered Nurse since 1993 working in settings including critical care units, emergency departments, and home health. I became a Psychiatric Nurse Practitioner and Clinical Nurse Specialist in 2003 and have practiced in diverse outpatient settings from California to Virginia in a large psychiatric practice, a residential setting, and a clinic for low–income uninsured patients. These experiences have given me a unique perspective about the limitations of some of our evidence–based practices.

I questioned whether we were truly helping as many people as we could with evaluations during fast paced interactions, disease management, and medication. Tightly booked appointments, rushing from one patient to the next, and using medical terms to categorize natural reactions to complex life circumstances did not sit well with me and still does not to this day. Human complexities require respectful consideration so that our efforts to heal don't dehumanize practitioners or patients or lead us to lose sight of the very essence of our being – *our soul*. Therefore, I wrote this book to share concepts, teach, educate, empower, strengthen, cultivate, and foster personal growth and development for all people.

Life is a learning journey.

One of the things I've learned along my journey is the roles we participate in can help us evolve yet it's important to see where our roles can limit us. I have formal education and training; however, countless informal teachers have taught me so much and they continue to reveal to me that there is more to learn. Each patient I have met with, people who came into my life as family members, friends, co–workers, or subject matter experts, and people who are different from me have been, and continue to be, my informal teachers.

It is tempting to maintain a belief or mindset, but I've learned that rigidness provides a false sense of security. There are certain things that simply are: the sky is blue, grass is green, water is wet, fire is hot, living humans breathe air; however, there are things I'm sure of which can be transformed by the next conversation, glance, or interaction that shows up in my life. I have personally benefitted from keeping an open mind about the many ways to experience and perceive life.

The teaching and suggestions reflected upon in this book are centuries old. Thousands of books about paths to inner peace and happiness have been written yet so many people continue to struggle. If we continue to believe that our own lack of peace and happiness is dependent on the actions of another person or on certain experiences, the cycle of misery will continue.

As a Psychiatric Nurse Practitioner and Clinical Nurse Specialist, I have met with people ranging from ages 5 to 90-year-old in a variety of clinical settings. On average, I've had 10–20 face to face encounters, 5 days a week, since 2003. I've met with people who are male, female, Black, White, Hispanic, Asian, Middle Eastern, European, Jewish, Christian, Muslim, Buddhist, Atheist, Agnostic, Hindu, Wiccan, Satanist, Pagan, rich, poor, highly educated, unschooled, homosexual, heterosexual, hypersexual, metrosexual, pansexual, transgender, transvestite, people who suffered horrifying abuse and people who simply needed to be heard. I have not met one person who isn't longing for happiness, peace, confidence, respect, understanding, compassion, and grace.

In this writing, I will attempt to reflect upon patterns I've observed to help you find your own way towards peace and happiness. If you integrate the concepts written in this book into your life, you can anticipate improved confidence, connectedness, a personal sense of security and peace as you develop clarity about the way *emotion, mind, ego,* and *spirit* influence our lives.

Chapter 1 Setting the Stage

Imagine that before coming to Earth, we were all
sitting in a meeting place on the other side... unbound by a
mind, an ego, or emotions. Instead, we were operating in
the fullness of the soul and the very essence of who we are
(our spirit). While in that state of being, we could not
imagine anything that could overpower such boundless
love, wisdom, peace, joy, kindness, patience, gentleness,
and self–control.

Though we receive a warning about the power of
the mind, the power of the ego, ever changing emotions,
and the countless temptations we'll encounter, it seems

unimaginable that anything could override such beauty and the reality of who we are.

Then we arrive. *We are born.*

The conditioning starts because we are raised by people who have already been programmed in ways that have overridden their own knowledge and remembrance of the very essence of who they are.

This is a universal cycle...

Chapter 2 Do You Have a Label?

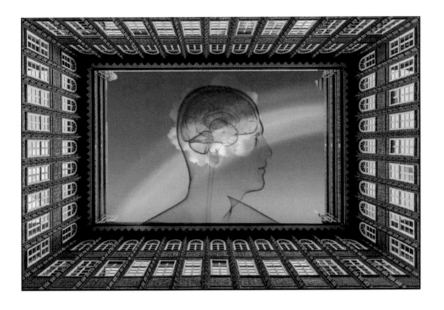

We have constructed a system of labeling people who report fear, sadness, worry, or anger with "disorders"; but humans are complex and there are many variables that can create symptoms. If we quickly conclude that the symptoms are based on physiology alone, we risk missing out on key issues that medical interventions cannot address. We tend to label people as "sick" when they get caught in a cycle of fear, judgment, abandonment, rejection, or various forms of abuse, instead of viewing their symptoms as a natural consequence of their life circumstances.

Influencers of our health and well–being are intertwined. Consider the quality of your sleep and your diet – including your consumption of non–nutritional items such as nicotine, drugs, alcohol, and food additives, and the amount of exercise you get. Think about the types of stressors you are exposed to. Stressors include major life events such as buying a new home, marriage or divorce, the birth of a child, or the death of a loved one; but they also include weekly work commitments, daily domestic duties, and family or relationship challenges. You may not even recognize the latter as stressors because they are part of your everyday life, but they have a major impact on your overall health.

What about the negative stressors – the ones which cause fear, sadness, worry, or anger? If the cost of staying in a job or maintaining a relationship is to sacrifice your own thoughts, feelings, or opinions, then it's time to seriously evaluate the importance of that relationship or job. Why are you staying in a relationship with someone who will not listen to you, or who does not seem to be willing to change a behavior which causes you pain? Why work with an employer who undervalues your contributions or undermines your self–esteem?

Why do people endure this? I have heard these reasons:

I don't want to be alone...
I've invested a lot of time in this relationship...
It's family and they need me...
I need this job...
The financial security is important...

Our society holds the assumption that most of us have the skills to manage these types of experiences and the associated fear, sadness, worry, or anger. There is also an assumption that these skills are taught within our families and that highly educated and wealthy people have better coping skills. It has been my experience that coping skills are not based on traditional education, level of intelligence, or financial stability, but instead, on a willingness to look inside ourselves.

Chapter 3 The Basics

As we walk through this book together, I will reference a few terms and concepts that you may be unfamiliar with:

- The Four Zones:
  1. Emotion Zone
  2. Mind Zone
  3. Ego Zone
  4. Spirit Zone
- Energy Field
- Residuals
- Energy Work

Emotion Zone:

The *Emotion Zone* consists of the feelings we experience as things happen around us.

The Mind Zone:

The *Mind Zone* is filled with thoughts and constant internalized debating. For many, it's typically a very busy place. For others, the *Mind Zone* may seem "off" or "empty".

The Ego Zone:

The *Ego Zone* never forgets anything or lets anything go. It formulates strong defenses to protect us from betrayal and other types of harm. Internal dialogues in the *Ego Zone* include statements like, "Nobody will ever do that to me again!", "These people are mean and can't be trusted!", and " I'm right and they're wrong!". The *Ego Zone* is judgmental, harsh, and argumentative.

The Spirit Zone:

The *Spirit Zone* can mean *Intuition, Gut Feeling, God, The Holy Spirit, Higher Self, Goddess, Divinity, Energy, The Universe, Sub–Conscious, "The Part of Me that Knows Better", Spiritual Law, Universal Law, Karma,* or *Instinct.*

There is no rigid definition of the *Spirit Zone* and there are no limitations because it is *the essence of who you are.*

The *Emotion, Mind, Ego,* and *Spirit* are aspects of ourselves that can't be removed or even completely turned off. Life is a series of experiences and one of the choices you have in the moment of each experience is which zone serves as your primary driver – The *Ego Zone, Emotion Zone, Mind* Zone, or *Spirit Zone.*

Characteristics of the Four Zones: Emotion, Mind, Ego, and Spirit

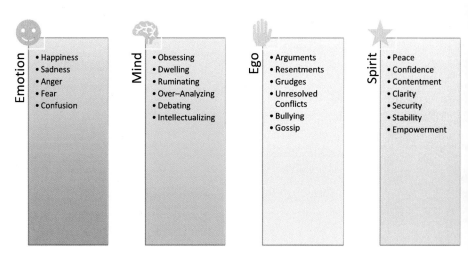

Emotion	Mind	Ego	Spirit
• Happiness • Sadness • Anger • Fear • Confusion	• Obsessing • Dwelling • Ruminating • Over–Analyzing • Debating • Intellectualizing	• Arguments • Resentments • Grudges • Unresolved Conflicts • Bullying • Gossip	• Peace • Confidence • Contentment • Clarity • Security • Stability • Empowerment

Figure 3-1

The Four Zones inside you – Emotion, Mind, Ego, and Spirit

Figure 3-2

Figure 3-3

Energy Field:

Think of your *Energy Field* as your "Aura" or "Vibration". It's influenced by your experiences and current state and how you manage them.

Residuals and Energy Work:

Residuals are the emotional impact of your experiences. *Residuals* can be positive or negative. They affect your thoughts and emotions constantly, so they quickly become the conditioning or programming inside your life.

Certain experiences can lead to painful memories which result in negative *Residuals*. It isn't possible to erase your memories, but it is possible to diminish and remove negative *Residuals* by cleansing your *Energy Field.* This is called *Energy Work* and, if you can do this, you will experience peace of mind and emotional stability.

Let's delve deeper now that you have a basic understanding of these terms and concepts and how they fit together – *Emotion Zone, Mind Zone, Ego Zone, Spirit Zone, Energy Field, Residuals,* and *Energy Work.*

Chapter 4 Triggers

The answers are inside you.

Often we claim to be "over" past events. Yet when we experience a similar situation or circumstance, we feel pain. In other words, you're not only dealing with a current situation, you feel the emotions from the past scenarios. As a society, we are not well adapted to or equipped to know how to separate our emotions and ego from memories – especially when it comes to harmful experiences. To optimize what can be gained from this book, you must actively acknowledge that you have Residuals in your Energy Field and you must be willing to understand how Energy Work is central to healing.

The following image shows how your Energy Field interacts with another person's Energy Field. For example, if your Energy Field is filled with negative Residuals, and you interact with another person whose Energy Field is also filled with negative Residuals, you'll both magnify those negative Residuals. You will trigger each other. These triggers are reminders of what still needs to be cleansed from your Energy Field.

Interaction between two Energy Fields with Negative Residuals

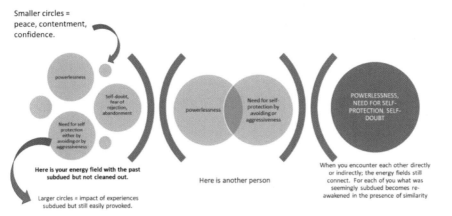

Figure 4-1

Without conscious and deliberate *Energy Work*, you'll tend to use avoidance or over–processing. You may even project what you are trying to avoid inside yourself onto other people.

The next shows how things look if negative *Residuals* have been cleansed from your *Energy Field*. This is not to say that your *Energy Field* will ever be completely clean, but you can create a predominantly clean *Energy Field*. When your *Energy Field* is predominantly clean, you'll be better equipped to manage what you encounter from another person's *Energy Field* or whatever else may trigger you.

Interaction between two Energy Fields when one Energy Field is clean

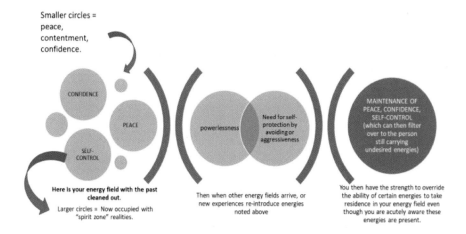

Figure 4-2

Attending to your Energy Field consciously and continuously is necessary because energy exchange is constant. You can choose what you allow to take residence in your Energy Field, and you can be thoughtful about what you are transmitting to other people. For example, if you encounter someone who has a great deal of anger in their Energy Field; rather than reacting to them with judgement, you can project thoughts of love and compassion towards them, creating an opportunity for them to shift away from

34

anger. Doing this can also help you stay out of the Ego Zone.

It can be easy to be buried beneath negative Residuals; however, if you balance the position of your mind, ego, and emotion and make your way back to the essence of who you are, which is the Spirit Zone, you'll view painful past experiences in a different way.

Being triggered can be used to unburden you.

Triggers can help you understand what needs to be cleansed from your Energy Field. To start putting this concept into action I invite you to ask yourself what's being triggered within you while you read this book. When you read a concept or example I've shared which offends or angers you, instead of making judgements, take a deep look at what has been triggered and begin the journey of Energy Work by releasing those residuals. Ask yourself, *"What patterns do I keep repeating in my life even though they do not serve me well?"* Notice whether you made a promise to yourself because of a difficult experience. Usually these promises come from the Ego Zone and they are a barrier to healing.

Consistently using triggers as an opportunity to free yourself and increase your personal power takes practice. As you read this book, focus on what's happening inside you.

What are the reactions from your emotions, ego, mind, and spirit?

Chapter 5 So It Starts from Day One?

The endless fear that exists among us tells me constantly that you, Spirit, might be wrong or worse yet, that you are wrong.

What is "it"?

"It" is the separation from the spirit zone that dwells in each of us.

We have all been children. Therefore, I'm inviting you to consider that we have all been indoctrinated with experiences in this life because that is what life is…one experience after another. In our childhood, we have even less control over what experiences befall us than we do in our adult life. At some point, we can ask ourselves what did the experiences teach us? And, what is my individual responsibility in how my experiences dictate current experiences in my life? And, through which zone will I interpret my experiences?

Yes, the responsibility lies on the individual. Blame does not help anybody move forward from their experience. Blame is birthed inside the ego and creates patterns that feel like protection, yet instead, perpetuates the pain of the experience in ways that are debilitating.

So, the invitation here is to look at experiences from a different perspective. Though it can be easily misconstrued that parents are being blamed for how their children turn out; again, I ask you to see the much bigger picture. All of us have been children. There are societal expectations and norms which we all fall into. If you are reading this, then you are at the very least curious about new ideas and ways of managing experiences.

Reflect on the possibility that children are often suffocated in our society by adults, systems, and rules. How then can we wonder why those children may not function well or perhaps over function in their childhood and then as they transition into adult life.

In the context of this material, "function well" equals:

- Having a sense of direction/passion/purpose
- Knowing how to name what they are experiencing
- Knowing how to communicate about their experiences and their actual vs. perceived experiences with openness and curiosity
- Understanding the way the body functions and communicates with us
- And, clear direction in how to navigate conflict rather than avoiding conflict

Are we a society that tells children who they must be instead of helping them discover who they are? When is the last time you responded to a child with respect when they expressed their thoughts, feelings, or opinions on something? How often have you seen expression from children perceived or judged as disrespectful? What is your memory of your childhood in this regard?

Why is it that when thoughts/feelings/opinions are vocalized from a child, it is not thought to be valued; but instead, it is considered "talking back", "sass", or "disrespect" to the adult. Maybe the child has some valuable thoughts and that is what is so threatening. Is this not an opportunity to explore with the child? In reality, if the adult was not given this respect in their childhood, then often similar or opposite spectrum patterns occur. What is meant here is that I've witnessed situations where if an adult had major restrictions as a child; they might go to an opposite extreme and not create adequate structure or boundaries for their own children. Or, a parent might repeat the pattern of being overly restrictive with their children. Important also to consider is that even though the adult might have excellent awareness in their parenting techniques; if they remain conflicted inside themselves about their own childhood experience, this can filter over to the child because of how our Energy Field dynamics exchange constantly with or without our awareness.

Over and over as I've met with people, I've noticed a pattern of not teaching children how to express themselves by giving them the words they need to describe what they feel around them and internally. Why have we as a culture so easily and readily dismissed energy exchange? Do we really think a child does not feel what is happening around them? Just because they do not have the vocabulary at the time does not mean they are not experiencing it. If we do not give the vocabulary, we are creating a mixed message early about how to interpret what is being felt around them. Think about it. We know a child can feel hot or cold, if something is too tight, hunger, pain, and fatigue. How is it that we are convincing ourselves that we are not to burden children with "adult" feelings like anger, insecurity, doubts, fears, anxiety, and so on. Imagine the empowerment if we were to teach children very early how to identify exactly what they are experiencing. This approach would certainly hold all of us more accountable.

It is easy to teach about colors, counting, and the alphabet as this is less threatening. Are we not inadvertently giving a conflicting message in our efforts to hide certain aspects of ourselves from other family members and children in particular? Does this not set the stage for a child to be more vulnerable and gullible? If children learn early to trust what they are sensing, the development of discernment becomes a powerful protective spirit zone mechanism. The fact that we live in a world where people do deceive and lie; trusting oneself and development of discernment are necessary protective mechanisms. Therefore, we are not only giving this skill so they will have their own descriptors for what they are experiencing but so they can properly discern what they are perceiving around them. Most are familiar with the saying "the anger is so thick in here you could cut it with a knife" even though everyone is smiling and trying to hide it.

Imagine a world where children know what they are sensing around them. So much less gullible then. So much more confident. Much less likely to be persuaded into choices they may not really want to have any part of. Imagine ALL members of a household being accountable for their own choices. What happens far too often based on patterns I've witnessed is that from birth most of us are trained to not listen to our own instinct. We are not validated in what we feel around us and how our body receives that.

For example, deception in the room can show up as indigestion. Anger in the room can show up as a cold sensation. Being that we all look for formulas or absolutes; I must say that there is no absolute to how any one person will be alerted by their intuition. Plenty may experience deception and anger as alerts from the body and others may simply "know" something is off even though they cannot explain it and even though they are told they are wrong if they choose to ask/confront. To avoid being misled, we must be taught to value and trust what we are sensing and feeling from the moment we get here and from the moment we seek to make connections and communicate in the context of this world. Perhaps this is why people are otherwise so easy to fall prey to deception, to being taken advantage of, to being lured into activity that they otherwise could perhaps have noticed alarms going off inside themselves to redirect their course. Just because we ask about something doesn't mean the other person will acknowledge it.

Our accepted parenting and the parenting that goes on behind closed doors tends to negate the intuition in a person. Children are generally not taught to listen to what they perceive around them. Instead, children are taught that they are only children and should go play, stay out of adult business, or simply do as they are told without any consideration to the development, they need to navigate such a confusing world. Of course children do not need to be included in details of adult squabbles or issues; but, if a child senses something is wrong, the parent can safely validate for them whatever they are feeling/perceiving. For example: Mommy is feeling afraid right now. This is what fear feels like. Or anger, or confusion, or excitement, or whatever the feeling might be. The opposite typically happens...... "I'm fine. Now you just go play. This is adult stuff. It's none of your business." So a child never learns what he/she is perceiving and then becomes gullible to whatever someone says instead of to what he/she perceives.

Have you ever given your child a chance to say what he/she thinks or perceives?

Have you ever put serious thought into what they do have to contribute?

Was this done for you?

If not, what residuals has this created for you?

Chapter 6 Conditioning/Programming

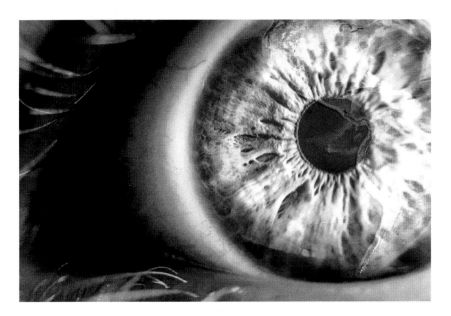

I've heard people say they do not want to be brainwashed and then avoid particular groups. Let me suggest that we are all being brain washed (programmed and conditioned) by all our encounters every day unless we address these experiences from the wisdom of the Spirit zone. See next image for deeper explanation.

Going back to, "we have all been children".

Life Experiences create perceptions

Formulates both desired and undesired habits/patterns

Life experiences can be interpreted by emotion and ego

Or life experiences can be interpreted through spirit zone and then "cleansed" so does not create undesired habits/patterns

Figure 6-1

When we hear it, but do not internalize it

Figure 6-2

When we negatively internalize what other people say

Figure 6-3

Conditioning - conditioning starts from the moment you get here. Whatever you grow up with you decide is normal. If those around you tell you there is something wrong with you, far too often you believe it. The judgements and accusations of others (that are projections from their ego zone) far too often create self–doubt (which is the first clue that it is a projection of any zone other than spirit zone). How do I know this? Because spirit zone does not direct your path with shame, guilt, embarrassment, or humiliation. Those are outcomes of ego zone. Spirit zone redirection is experienced as an "A–ha", as relief even when you suddenly become aware of something you need to change about your own behavior. Spirit zone elicits awareness and an eagerness to change because of the awareness. As you are relating toward others and from others out of ego zone, perceptions and emotions can very quickly become quite twisted and complicated. Spirit zone solutions are typically addressing the current situation and not as futuristic.

The clear-cut answer is to aim to operate from spirit zone which typically does not align with ego zone but will lead you to your goal one step at a time. We are so accustomed to ego zone that following anything otherwise begins to feel unnatural or like you are letting someone get away with something because there is not a "fight" involved. Here is where you must repeatedly experience the power inside the spirit zone. It does not matter how much I write about how powerful it is; you must experience that for yourself. Herein lies the challenge. People want instantaneous results, instantaneous "feel good" or the tool being "tested" is immediately judged to be no good. Learning to live in spirit zone is an arduous task, requires constant intention, and does not happen overnight. In other words, transitioning into and trusting the process of spirit zone does not happen without determination, discipline, and practice, practice, practice. Remember, following ego has become the "norm" or "more natural" feeling of power; so following spirit zone may or may not "feel" powerful right away. For those of you who might be concerned, spirit zone does NOT equal being a doormat. Quite the opposite.

It is important to add here that just because someone participates in religious groups or claims certain religious beliefs does not equal walking in spirit zone. There has been teaching for centuries to guide us into higher functioning and awareness. Regardless, we seem to perpetually derail from the very teaching that can create and satisfy our inner most yearnings and move us closer to our spirit zone. Because the conditioning starts from day one, many may not find their way back to their own spirit zone.

Does anyone tell the truth? Does anyone really know how to kindly say what they are thinking as they are experiencing an interaction with someone? Where did we learn that it is not okay to interact with honesty?

Somewhere, it got instructed (in childhood) that you have to be "nice" by simply agreeing with people. It is common teaching to not tell someone you are uncomfortable with or disagree with something they have said or done. Here is where it gets very tangled. Somehow our societal norms justify that it is acceptable to turn around and say what you really think to someone else and act as if there is no cost to this choice. Projections begin as one experience after another is not diffused in the context of the original experience. It then shows up in other ways such as interacting with everyone angrily, becoming anxious, becoming depressed, entering into obsessive thinking or sleep disruption because you internalized the experience instead of saying what you think to the person it needed to be spoken to. This is where we become teachers for each other in all our interactions. Adults, some knowingly and others unknowingly, teach a child that their opinion doesn't matter until they are an adult. Adults then are unpracticed at how to do confrontation constructively. Constructively equals without name calling, without defensiveness, with compassion, with directness, and with clarity but no harshness.

Power is not in becoming angry, gossiping, being vindictive, or in seeking payback; but instead to simply stand in honesty. How is it that we live in a society that protects the people bringing harm (unless it is criminal and even sometimes then)? Examples I think of are in everyday occurrences such as: a boss who is impossible to relate to, a co–worker who is mean or rude (yet they do good work) making others miserable, people in leadership positions with poor leadership skills, and "there's always one" whether in the family, church, or community. I've witnessed both individuals and groups that remain afraid to confront "the one" who is doing the harm. Then we wonder why extreme responses occur. We do not need to make everything a judicial issue. We need to stand up as individuals, groups, or in whatever number of people it takes to demonstrate that we are serious about not allowing unacceptable interactions, intentional or not.

Am I trying to create a society that has no diversity or that does not allow differences of perceptions? No way and quite the opposite. I would like to think that diversity can be embraced without harmful reactions or judgement. I think of the people I've talked to who might present with high anxiety or feelings of depression only to discover over time that part of the problem is learning to live in a society that has such hatred and disdain for who they are, perhaps an individual with same sex preferences. This, in no way, is a conclusion that if a person has anxiety or depression, it is due to hiding their sexual preference. However, there is typically some level of "hiding" experiences or perceptions that are very deep and personal with no seeming "safe" place to sort through what is being concealed for far too many people. If people are living in the fullness of who they are, which they can only discover if they have been given the freedom to live within their own intuition and not within the control of limited perceptions, most likely there can be growth in achieving differences without judgement.

Do you know how to discuss deep matters of the heart inside your family unit? If you do not know how to talk in your most personal, intimate relationships, then it is less fulfilling what you accomplish on a larger scale. You can be capable of being a communicator in a system (large or small) and gain a sense of satisfaction and cooperation; but until that is gained in a deep, personal manner there is tendency to be discontent.

Look at conditioning and programming from this perspective in consideration to this scale:

Here's the Challenge

Looking at experiences on a scale of 1-10 with 1 being abusive and 10 being no form of abuse.

1	2	3	4	5	6	7	8	9	10

Identifying the scale

1 = repeated physical, emotional, sexual abuse

2 = periodic incidents of physical, emotional, sexual abuse.

3 = rare incidents of physical, emotional, sexual abuse

4 = periodic physical or emotional abuse or both

5 = periodic emotional abuse

6 = rare emotional abuse

7 = no further abuse and actively striving for self-actualization, conflict resolution, honesty, trust, peace

8 -10 May seem unattainable to those in 1-4 range or even undesired as may seem "snooty". Process of respect, conflict resolution, honesty, trust, peace

Figure 6-4

If you have been raised in a 1–3 range, that seems "normal" to you and 4–5 can look *really good* even though it is still demoralizing. If conditioned somewhere in the 1–5 range, reaching 8–10 range can seem undesirable as that range can be misconstrued as "they think they are better than us" or it can just seem simply impossible due to the strain of the conditioned tolerance. Material needs met does not equal emotional and psychological needs met. Higher Education does not equal emotional and psychological health.

Chapter 7 Drowning in My Experiences

Our cultural conditioning can lead us into "drowning in our experiences". Suffering shows up in so many forms and is something we naturally seek to avoid at all costs. Oddly, it seems that the more we try to run from the suffering, the more we suffer. Another favorite quote: "Perhaps the only pain that can be avoided in life is the pain that comes from trying to avoid pain" by R.D. Laing.

In my years of trying to save myself from my own suffering and in trying to help others find those solutions that minimize their suffering, I've seen repeated common themes. Again, I would suggest that "It" is our forgetfulness of the spiritual zone aspect of ourselves that amplifies any suffering we encounter while here. We have many paths in our society to awaken, support, teach, comfort, and equip people to get through life. Some of these paths seem to actively further the paralysis of dealing with pain in life rather than moving you out of and beyond your pain and suffering. Though the onset of emotional pain and suffering cannot be stopped, getting stuck in that pain and suffering can be controlled.

Emotional pain and suffering start in the ego and emotions and can eventually take a toll on the body and completely drown out the awareness of spirit zone. Though you cannot prevent certain experiences, you can empower yourself to not let the experiences rob even an extra day much less 20, 30, 40, 50 years!

Figure 7-1

It does not seem to work consistently to use the mind to control the ego or the emotions as this can quickly turn into an obsessive cycle of sorts. Instead, by finding spirit zone, you are then able to have the opportunity to stop participating in the chaos the ego and emotions create.

We cannot remove mind or ego—nor do we want to as they serve a purpose in their proper position. If mind or ego shifts to the larger cog, rest is much harder to gain.

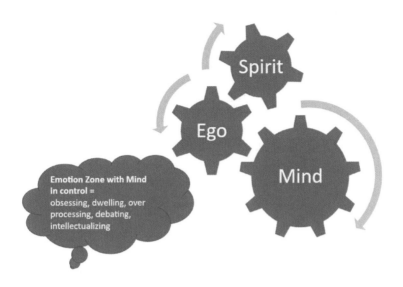

Figure 7-2

I've found it both rewarding and disheartening to be in a professional role where I can help another search for that delicate balance in what psychotropic medication can do for the person suffering versus what is about individual skill building and equipping a person who has been improperly conditioned or prepared for what life brings their way. It has been rewarding as individual by individual, that awakening is created.

It is disheartening when it seems the mechanisms of the larger system designed to bring help often doesn't place much value to this type of teaching. Perhaps if for no other reason due to productivity demands. Instead, there may even be a thread of cynicism about this more mystical aspect of ourselves. It seems as though this perpetual avoidance of spirit zone or leaving spirit zone health up to religious groups only, can in some instances further perpetuate the suffering. And again, religious activity does not equal spirit zone awareness.

Figure 7-3

Chapter 8 Removing the Barrier of Defensiveness

If there was anything I could immediately relieve people of, it would be the habit of defending yourself.

Interesting how it is, but those who are most defensive typically are the first to say, "I'm not defensive". I think rather than going on a dissertation about removing defensiveness, I would like to invite each reader to apply the concepts inside this book. Then examine for yourself what happens to any inclination of defensiveness inside yourself and how you see defensiveness in those around you.

Early in my professional role, I had this youthful idea that people just need to be taught to communicate and upon receiving that teaching, they would flourish in their communication and therefore in their relationships. I had no idea the resistance I would meet to this simple teaching of communication when the communication was about more than the weather, movies, or sports. Regardless, resistance around communication does not make communication any less important. In a later chapter, there will be discussion of how avoiding efforts to communicate comes with a cost.

We have all heard, experienced, and participated in the resistance of communication in one form or another. Our very existence is complex and the multitude of defense mechanisms we have so blindly fallen into as a means of self–protection hinder the only real protection that can be found from the insights inside the spirit zone.

The next pages show a few examples of statements people make as both conscious and unconscious efforts to avoid direct conversation that is required to address uncomfortable circumstances. What is meant by "unconscious efforts"? A person is not likely consciously thinking "what is the best way for me to get around this". It is simply a conditioned response that has been created from patterns of avoidance that exist throughout our society, and hence, is a default setting that likely feels very practical, important, and correct.

Common Examples

1. You're the crazy one, not me. Go to your shrink.
2. You need some medication or something. Go to your doctor.
3. You're hurting me. (when trying to address a pertinent uncomfortable issue)
4. You're attacking me. (when trying to address a pertinent uncomfortable issue)
5. Not right now. (only for the "right" time to not show up)
6. You can never let anything go.
7. Nobody is perfect.
8. You think you're better than us, don't you?
9. Confronting with statements that are dismissive, critical, or misconstrue without willingness to clarify or seek to understand.

10. Immersion in "Good" distractions without returning to issues that need resolving. (work, community service, church, sports, hobbies)
11. Blatant refusal to talk about the topic on the table.
12. Avoidance tactics in general.
13. People cope differently.
14. Don't give me that psychobabble.

Children are often told the above and these additionally

15. Don't talk back to me like that.
16. Don't disrespect me like that.
17. Go play, these are adult issues without any education about how to give words to what they are feeling in the room. (As discussed in Chapter 5)
18. Being forced to believe that there is only one way to think about things and identified as rebellious if has questions that challenge the belief.
19. Being forced to explain behavior as a measure to determine whether "Punishment" will occur.

I invite you to observe the degree of defensiveness in which people respond in efforts to communicate, and how this is draining and unproductive. Observe how often people are not listening to what is being said, but instead are responding like children being chided by a parent. Hard sentence to write, but too many adults carry this over from their childhood.

Why are children being addressed in a way that creates defensiveness rather than critical thinking?

Can we not see that it is not working to put any person at any age in a position that they feel they have to defend themselves?

Where is the conversation, the negotiation, the debate, the accountability, the taking responsibility for behaviors and words?

Why is there punishment, judgement, or criticism rather than natural consequence?

Am I able to receive feedback without getting defensive?

Chapter 9 Tired of Tiptoeing: Let's March Instead

In all of my efforts to say what I mean, my story gets tangled in your story. My ego fights but my spirit resolves.

In this current age of such incredibly advanced technology, many seem convinced that we are communicating and connecting through this technology. Yet, the same problem continues to exist. A resistance to direct, honest communication disciplined with the ability to redirect oneself from ego zone and occupy spirit zone to get the best outcomes out of the communication exchange.

Has this world ever been a place where people can talk? Have people really been able sit down and talk through differences? Have we ever accomplished circles where the majority stop judging, stop criticizing, stop ridiculing, stop rejecting, stop abandoning other people or oneself in order to truly operate in love, acceptance, and compassion? We say the words, but do the behaviors line up?

How is it that we have become a people who are afraid to say to the person across from you what you really think or feel about what they have said? How is it that instead we have become a people who tells Person B the problem you have with Person A instead of speaking straight to Person A? How is it that we came to believe such dishonesty would not create sickness inside the soul and eventually to the body by denying such a fundamentally important aspect of our human nature?

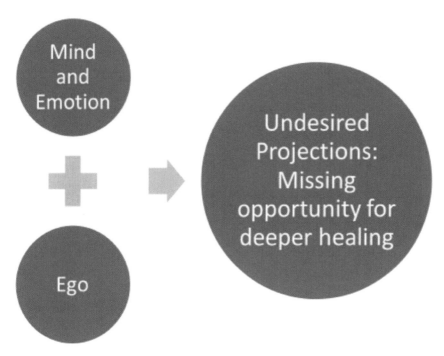

Figure 9-1

Let's look at different examples of choices as you experience different types of communication encounters:

Track 1: The person communicating with you has no conscious awareness of how what they said was received by you. Their intention was to share a thought or feeling but suddenly you find yourself filled with intense emotions and thoughts about what was said or by how it was stated. Your choices:

1. Reveal what you are experiencing from your own flood of ego and emotion.

2. Or, reveal what you are experiencing but from spirit zone.

3. Or, from concepts taught inside the book, see the other person as your "teacher" in that they triggered something "undesired" inside you which you also now have a choice to either simply keep to yourself and meditate upon for the sake of releasing which then changes the perspective of the encounter.

4. Or, a combination of #2 and #3.

Track 2: The person was consciously aiming to jab at you. Your choices:

1. Respond from ego zone which will likely turn into an argument.

2. Ignore the jab and then talk about it to someone else which is also ego zone.

3. Respond from spirit zone which helps the matter resolve <u>inside you</u> more readily even if resolve between the parties participating is not accomplished. Realistically we cannot control the outcome for other people, we can only choose which zone we respond from and trust that spirit zone is most productive whether we get the privilege of witnessing that in the life of the other person or not.

Track 3: The person is relating to you from ego zone without any concern as to how what they are saying is coming across or affecting you.
Your choices:

1. Lead by example through spirit zone relating.

2. You may have to separate yourself from this type of person if there is absolute refusal to consider other ways of relating. Meeting this person from your own ego zone will likely illicit a maddening cycle of arguing. Additionally, meeting them from spirit zone does not guarantee they will allow themselves to take the risk of trusting that process.

3. Observe "the cost" of staying in this type of relationship

Track 4: The person is relating to you from ego zone without any awareness of any other choice; but would be receptive to knowing how they have affected you.
1. Lead by example through spirit zone relating.
2. In all Tracks, always ask yourself what is being learned in the exchange.

***Reminders about Spirit Zone: NOT a doormat, NOT aggressive but clear & direct, powerful without aggression, articulates emotion without impulsivity of emotion*

There seems to be two extremes of emotional expression that happen without much thought:
1. Minimal expression, keeping most things to oneself acting as if "everything's fine", the good ole "nothing" when asked what's going on?
2. Emotional blasting with tears or anger or shear manipulation that plays on the emotions of another person.

Consider that behaviors of acting either aggressively (blasting) or passively (silence) are ego zone default settings created from conditioning and experiences. These do not seem to be conscious choices but instead deeply ingrained programming that has simply been accepted. Unfortunately, even ego zone ways of coping work to some degree depending on the situation.

The Question: How do you shift this programming?

Each of us has different experiences that influence what we hear and how we say things. If we find ourselves reacting with hurt, anger, or pain from something that was said and we do not take the time to clarify if what we heard is what they intended for us to hear, then another preventable vicious cycle ensues. Is it best practice to assume what someone means by what they say? It is true that there are people who will not respond when we seek to clarify or who may respond defensively or rudely (which is coming from where in them... yes, the ego zone). Most people have experienced some sort of wounding and may be so far removed from spirit zone that any effort to approach that zone with them can erroneously feel like an intrusion and violation.

Once again, if we approach that person from ego zone, there is less opportunity for productive results. Going to someone from spirit zone does not guarantee they will seek or find their own spirit zone. But again, we can only be accountable for our own actions. This is a very important statement. Our intention should never be to relate to someone from spirit zone to elicit anything from them. That would not be spirit zone as that is another form of manipulation.

Catering to the ego zone of another will take a big toll on the persons doing the catering. Obviously, if there are issues of safety at hand, help must be sought as to how to safely bring resolve to that situation. The person operating from ego zone is no less accountable for their actions. Ego driven actions can absolutely be intimidating and can control the entire atmosphere occupied. Avoid giving those who operate from ego driven perspectives power over and over to dictate the atmosphere of the environment and creating an atmosphere that is uneasy for all those around. Be very conscientious of how that ego zone behavior is inadvertently forcing you to maneuver yourself.

Characteristics of Productive Conversation

Honesty spoken with respect and consideration, non–defensive, eager to hear non–defensive responses, eager to hear honesty from others

Characteristics of Non–Productive Conversation

Defensive, stifling, shaming, harsh vs. constructive criticism, accusatory, silence

Both productive and non–productive conversation can create anxious responses and uncomfortable feelings in your body and in your emotions. So, discernment is the key. *Did the conversation produce insights and sharpen awareness? Did it broaden your experiences or was it limiting?*

Remember that communication can be complicated to some and takes a lot of energy. Remember the sentence you formulate may make perfect sense to you, but the person who hears it does not hear it the way you intended. Consider that your brain produces so many thoughts and so many interpretations primarily based on your own personal experiences and how you managed those experiences.

We each have unique personal experiences and perceptions of the same experience; therefore, you can have many interpretations of a single thought. It seems we take for granted that most people assume the person who formulated the sentence meant it the way you took it… especially when it feels hurtful or harmful. *Can you begin to consider that the other person did not mean to hurt you? That instead they simply do not know the story going on inside your own experience(s) that would create the interpretation you have made?* Regardless, it is still important to clarify in these instances as this is how each person comes to a better understanding of the other.

An example in my own life that I will never forget. And, I will not forget it because the person had the confidence to come back and tell me how she heard what I said. I was so thankful because it was not what I was trying to say.

My statement was something along the lines of, "I'll always have a job because our society doesn't know how to emotionally support people". Now, the story inside my head was around feelings of exasperation that so many people suffer because so many people avoid or distract from any unpleasant emotion rather than supporting each other in walking through their pain. For example, someone going through a divorce. The solution to the loneliness and sadness of the broken relationship turns into, "Just go out for dinner or coffee with someone else" instead of validation of the complexity of the feelings.

What the person I spoke to heard was that I sounded arrogant. It was insulting to her when I meant for it to validate that she is not broken, but our society is. That was a huge lesson for me to realize how my best intentions can be harmful without me realizing it because my sentence can only make total sense within the context of my own thoughts and experiences. It saddens me to think of the number of times I hurt someone, and they did not tell me.

Therefore, is it not essential that we consistently seek to clarify at least in situations where the communication did not feel good. Yes, it is a lot of work to consciously monitor this. In the long run, it will build our connection with people. There will be more peace and understanding, less hatred/grudges/conflict, and perhaps more clarity of who to stay in relationship with or not. Of course, if the person was meaning to hurt you, then it is a different path of management.

Have people who refuse to consider your perspective or who refuse to carry conversation through to resolve succeeded at convincing you something is wrong with you? Again, being held accountable does not guarantee insight on their part; but it can shift the toll that ego driven behaviors place on you. Why can't we just talk? Learn from each other? Seek to understand? This is what psychology teaches us and people want to call that psychobabble?

Chapter 10 There is a Cost

My spirit speaks, but do I listen? How long will I abandon you, my spirit, and suffer that pain before I realize your help has always been with me?

I want to invite us to consider the behaviors we choose to participate in that are rooted in the ego zone come with a cost. Let me explain. Ego zone responses might look something like the following:

- Walking away from another person as if they do not matter.
- Refusing to have a rational conversation and see it all the way through. What is meant by "see it all the way through". I've rarely seen anything resolve with one conversation. Usually it takes a commitment of gathering and discussing followed with proper introspection until it settles. If it is not settling or the conversation stays the same, then each person needs to look inside themselves more deeply and honestly to see how to get the discussion progressing rather than staying stagnant.
- Not clarifying what a person meant by what was said especially when the words pierced something

inside you. As spoken in previous chapters, this is essential to be handled from spirit zone in order for the conversations to be effective. Ego responses are typically defensive or elicit defensiveness. Spirit zone will not only be seeking clarification but will also use the triggered experience as an opportunity to release the undesired vows/habits/patterns formulated from the experience and residuals that got triggered inside themselves.

- If I say something and it hurts you and you tell me and we each approach the opportunity from spirit zone, then deep healing and release can happen. The communication may need to occur several times and there must also be hard, honest introspection. The defensiveness (from ego zone) cannot be present for this to fully work in the context of the relationship; but neither person is dependent on the other to accomplish the opportunity for the internal release of what was triggered. If the hurt is addressed but from the position of ego zone, it will only perpetuate more hurt and link to more vows and more experiences from the past which then pull a person further away from their spirit zone.

I have witnessed people from all walks of life and all ages struggle with acknowledging their deeper struggles due to the constant judgement that circulates in our society. The judgement can often lead to feelings of shame which when internalized and allowed to remain hidden rather than released becomes yet another experience that drowns out the spirit zone.

What do I mean by deeper struggles? Mom or Dad having an affair and somehow you know but nobody else knows. Needing to tell someone that a behavior they choose is hurtful but in so doing you have so much fear it will hurt them or that they may lash out, you continue to internalize the hurt they project. Not speaking the words "I love you" or the other extreme of saying I love you but never resolving hurts or conflict and disrespect as long as it is chased with an "I love you". Have we talked about the cost of tolerating unresolved conflict and disrespect?

How is it that it can be going against the societal norm to be nice to another human being, to not gossip, to address issues through conversations (as messy as it might get), and to bring encouragement and acceptance into all encounters/relationships. How is it that we can wonder how there are so many symptoms (the cost) manifesting in countless different ways. Yet, we still grope for how to better treat the symptoms instead of seeking to resolve the conflicts inside our own lives from the space of spirit zone which can create the opportunity for positive ripple effects.

Before discussing the positive ripple effects of participating in spirit zone, I would like to discuss another very serious cost to accepting a default setting of ego zone. What we do in regards to behaviors we participate in, substances and foods we put in our bodies, the amount of sleep we get, the amount of exercise we get, the way we choose to discipline or not discipline ourselves has positive and negative impacts on the body and does manifest symptoms that are very real.

In this regard, I've witnessed the medical community being caught between a rock and a hard place as we live in such a litigious society where one's wellness or lack thereof is often blamed on someone else rather than regarded as a personal responsibility.

There is a very delicate and complicated balance therefore in what can be expected from such amazing scientific advancements, the impact of genetics, and what a person is doing or not doing that works against themselves. A clear-cut example is the person who is diabetic and chooses to indulge in sugar because they can take medicine. From the framework of this book, I'm suggesting that sometimes psychotropic medications are expected to compensate for lack of skills or refusal to participate in skills for one reason or another.

What science and technology have developed is unbelievable and to reap the benefits of such amazing developments is a gift of our time. The developments that have evolved to intervene for the health and safety of fellow human beings is AMAZING. But no matter the symptoms; the seeker of better health has to be undeniably accountable for their own behaviors on their body. It seems in our litigious society that this accountability has been lost. It seems there is an expectation that there is a medication and/or surgical intervention that will fix things those tools were never meant to fix. For example, a person may present with inability to sleep at night but not tell you they are sleeping all day or that they cannot sleep at night because of activity or emotional stress going on in the environment. There instead is a pressure to find a solution that will override the impact of all the stressors that are either denied or that one is unwilling to address or feels powerless to address.

No doubt there are people suffering from medical conditions/situations that the medical/scientific community has clearly and with astounding accomplishment developed interventions that could not have been dreamed of in years past. Let us keep up the development but let us not undermine the significance of the details being brought forth in this writing.

Thoughtful and thorough consideration must be given when determining why symptoms are present. There is a larger societal pitfall magnified by the fact that medical errors have occurred and the fact that caretakers can be sued.

It seems as though there is an overflow of psychiatric disease management in our society rather than disease prevention. Could this be due to people being lost in ego zone with little awareness of their own spirit zone? What type of difference would this awareness make on symptomatology?

Symptoms can only persist unless we each put forth tremendous effort to communicate honestly and to allow those around us to do the same. Though honesty does not always produce an individual's desired emotional or intellectual outcomes; the honesty will bring the clarity to help one search inside themselves as to what compels them in one direction or another based on the information in front of them at the time. Stepping out of emotional and ego driven responses inside ourselves expands our opportunity for a fuller life.

How does this tie into Projections?

I've witnessed and experienced from within myself and from others the cost of taking all my personal unresolved conflicts everywhere I go. Here is where we begin the discussion of projections. I will continue to break this down.

Chapter 11 The Impact of Projections

Other people are filtering over to you the impact of their experiences rather than dealing with you and only you in the context of that moment and current experience/interaction.

What are others sending out?

What are you sending out?

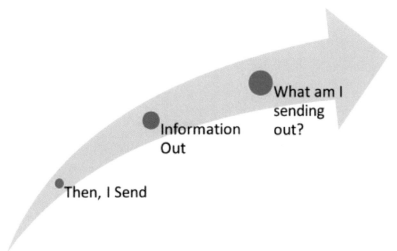

Figure 11-1

*"Everything changes when you start to **emit your own frequency** rather than absorbing the frequencies around you, when you start imprinting your intent on the universe rather than receiving an imprint from existence."*

Barbara Marciniak

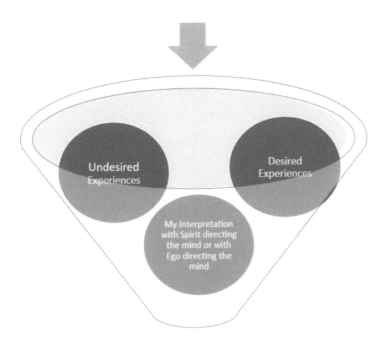

The PROJECTIONS I create and THE WAY I
INTERPRET EXPERIENCES

Figure 11-2

My best intentions can strike a wound deep inside someone so fiercely that it causes them to perceive me as an enemy rather than a friend, guide, or support person. For example: If someone is used to feeling chastised by family members, then suddenly my confrontation of certain behaviors to discuss openly and honestly becomes a replay of feelings of chastisement. If they don't tell me this, they leave feeling wounded or like I'm an enemy and they stay stuck in that residual effect in their life. The feeling of chastisement that started in previous experiences and was provoked by a current encounter then becomes the necessary trigger to give the opportunity to see more residual effects from past experiences that need releasing. The people who seek to clarify and use spirit zone to release the residual triggered are well on their way to a deeper healing inside themselves. (As discussed in Chapter 4)

Be aware to not absorb the pain that catapults itself upon you as others direct their defenses to you. Or perhaps the defenses are through avoiding and creating a world without you. Either way, pay attention to what is coming at you, so you don't absorb it and take it on. Here is where you can consider a protective type of meditation where you might create a "film" around yourself as a protective measure against the projections that are constantly occurring.

Dear spirit zone, may the force field of your power surround me and shield me so only good can enter.

Again, this is where a "trigger" is a gift as it is showing where further cleansing is needed inside your Energy Field. Also, consider the self–protection I speak of is different than a barricade. Protection is like the film you spray on carpet to protect from spills. Still approachable, no rough edges, yet nothing can penetrate and stain. You can see what is there from others attempting to take space in your Energy Field. Instead of allowing it to take space, you can respond inside yourself with gracious thoughts of love, healing, and peace to those who suffer. This takes constant decision making.

More Ways Projections are Assumed

- Always compensating for others
- Taking care of others needs before your own
- Being identified as the "bad guy" in efforts to address matters honestly
- Loss of empathy in pain of defending self
- Tolerance of harmful relationships

Chapter 12 Violations

You may steal a moment of my life, but it is my choice as to whether I allow you, violation, to have my entire life.

Here is another invitation to consider: because you have been violated does not mean your life is forever ruined. Far too often, people seem to get tangled within the impact of the ways in which they have been violated. Hence, losing sight of one's own strength, courage, or power (the spirit zone). The tangling creates an undesired perpetual violation of self by no longer engaging in the spirit zone due to "drowning in the experience". A beautiful example of an uncanny ability to face a situation from spirit zone is noted in a Documentary about the abduction and kidnapping of Natascha M. Kampusch.

Because in this world there will always be hatred, judgement, lying, cheating, stealing, sexual abuse, emotional abuse, and other violations, we can consider that our greatest defense is that of knowing how to trust our instinct and operate in spirit zone. It is a disservice to undermine the impact of everything we are inundated with if we are not going to properly equip ourselves with how to manage it. Being in a position of high intuitive awareness and spirit zone action does not guarantee a life without violation or hardships. It does guarantee the tools needed to manage any situation with which you are confronted in a way that does not pull you deeper into ego zone which is a certain path of misery. If you are in a car wreck because of a drunk driver and it changes your physical well–being forever, that situation will be much better managed from the insights of spirit zone than ego zone. Does managing it from spirit zone change if you gained a head injury or a missing limb? Of course not; however, it changes the way you address that challenge.

Violations can occur in a matter of seconds or can go on for years. Staying tangled inside the violation and the impact of the violation is where personal choice lies. We may not be able to prevent violation, but our spirit zone offers the best solution for management. This is likely a good place to look at concepts of forgiveness which I've seen misunderstood. *How?* I've seen people over time identify not forgiving as a source of internal power and control over the violator. Let us take a closer look and let us forget the word "forgive". Let us look at this from an Energy Field perspective. To hold onto any residual of a violation in any way leaves the experience sitting in your Energy Field ready to be triggered by anything that feels similar in any way. Ego zone convinces that "I will never forgive you" is power but this is an illusion.

From the perspective of this writing, we are seeking to stop all negotiations with illusions birthed in ego zone. Instead, it is by stepping into spirit zone that you will find all the tools you need to deal with the violations you have experienced. To get started, check in with your spirit zone. It is easier said than done.

You are a human being that experiences loss, betrayal, rejection, projections, manipulations, and so on. You likely have been conditioned to believe that these bad things should not happen. The problem is we live in a world where bad things do happen. The choice we have is to empower ourselves and to not let these events rob the rest of our lives.

Chapter 13 The Clues We are Given

You, spirit zone, whisper to me your wisdom. Then, I berate you when I do not listen and suffer those consequences.

I will address women first. This is relevant to all because of the cultural conditioning suggested here. Let us talk about the very real hormonal fluctuations and particularly the emotional symptoms associated with premenstrual syndrome otherwise known as PMS. Women: be cautious to not allow others to hide behind the label, "You're PMSing"? It seems to me that as human beings, we have beautiful barometers as part of our very existence. We are quickly taught to ignore the importance associated with these barometers. I invite women to start asking themselves a few questions.

What are the situations or circumstances that make you more irritable, less tolerant, less patient, or more apt to cry around the time of these hormonal shifts?

Are these circumstances/situations that you are generally tolerating inside your life otherwise?

Notice that I did not ask if these are situations you are fine with but situations you are tolerating.

Is there anything in your power that can be done about what you are tolerating that becomes intolerable around PMS time?

How often do you hear "you must be PMSing" as a defense mechanism for people to get out of the hot seat when they do not want to take responsibility for the contribution they are making in the situation?

Could this experience of PMS (at least in some situations) be a "signal" that there is something or perhaps many things not being tended to or not resolved in a satisfactory manner?

We have been conditioned to erroneously accept this signal as something wrong with ourselves instead of properly addressing issues in our lives that then leads to the barometer screaming from the inside of you as loud as possible to awaken you to do something different.

This is not to minimize that there are those who suffer with PMS and medication whether hormonal or SSRI's have provided necessary relief. This is not to minimize that post–partum depressions are hormonally driven and typically respond well to medication intervention. Hormonal changes create real symptoms but there are enough people that get lost in these labels that alternatives for management must also be considered.

How loud must the body scream before we listen? This is a question for all people.

I've had men and women tell me they feel like crying but do not in an effort to not feel weak as the illusion is taught. This construct applies especially to men. Men and women say they feel they have no one to talk to because others are busy, they do not want to be a burden, no one will listen, or people respond with pat answers. Men and women say they would never tell certain individuals what they really want to say (not because they are going to say it rudely) but because they do not want to take the risk of hurting feelings or experience possible repercussions for doing so. Some of the possible repercussions include being yelled at, cursed at, rejected, or emotionally abandoned in the process.

Men especially are conditioned to feel they cannot show different emotions due to the cultural labels that get placed on them from society. This is powerful conditioning when a person either intentionally does not listen to this wiser part of themselves or is not attuned to their spirit zone altogether.

Do you ever remember listening to this wiser part of yourself?

When did this stop or, worse yet, was that awareness ever there?

Here is the cost spoken of earlier. The cost to refrain from listening to the wiser self and to hold all this powerful energy inside creates feelings of heaviness, agitation, anxiousness, anger, depression, impatience, avoidance, hopelessness which can lead to other physical symptoms including headaches, pain, fatigue, nausea, vomiting, dizziness, and other symptoms. Here is where people get offended or feel like the medical system is failing them when tests are done by a doctor and there are no clear medical reasons to explain the symptoms. People feel accused that it is "all in your head". Over and over I've seen people get offended by the medical field not finding a medical explanation for their symptoms. I've watched these same people minimize any stress in their life.

The reality is that most of us are flailing along at managing stress and relationships. Consider the cost of eating sugar if you are a diabetic. Give similar consideration to daily stressors that can impact your mental health and even create unpleasant physical symptoms.

So why not accept that stress can cause physical symptoms that do not have medical explanations?

Stress can cause people to overeat which can lead to obesity, which can lead to high blood pressure, high cholesterol, and other such things.

Why do we think there is no cost to our body by the way we do or do not handle our experiences and relationships?

We have human bodies and they do break down over time. It is imperative not to ignore any clues the body is giving that disease resides inside you and to see any and all specialists needed in that regard. However, it is equally imperative to be careful while in this quest of finding medical answers that you do not forget and become inadvertently deterred from the intertwined effects of how the mind, body, spirit all work together. Far too often, we dismiss the fact that our body has physical symptoms to stress and emotional/psychological mismanagement of ourselves. Suddenly, people are covered with a multitude of labels that deters them from the very solution for which the body and soul are screaming. Consider the complexity of unexplained aches, pains, nausea, vomiting, GI upset, tension headaches, frequencies of migraine headaches, sleep problems, anxiety, depression, panic, and not to mention cutting, eating disorders, substance abuse, or seizure activity with a normal EEG. There is an intricate balance that physicians are constantly considering when it comes to running all appropriate tests to ensure that a disease is not being missed, not over testing, or helping a person accept that the problem is not biological in nature but rather from mismanagement of the essentials of our psychological and physiological needs. Additionally, there can be an imbalance of being referred to mental health specialists who also can get hyper focused on finding the biological solution and how to live with particular mental health diseases rather than assessing for and ensuring fundamental foundational skills are in place or to what degree these skills are intact. Even in the case of forthright mental health disease, a person is so much more than the disease and still has dire need (if not more urgently than others who are not susceptible to depression, anxiety, substance abuse and so forth) to have these foundational skills/insights sharply in place. Again, there seems to be so much resistance to the skill building especially when there are commercials that seductively create an idea there is a better, easier solution. Why? I invite you at this moment to not look at the larger systems as to why we may be stuck in this regard, but look inside yourself, find any and all resistance to trusting that spirit zone inside you and use meditation to allow any resistance to trusting your spirit zone to dissolve.

It is interesting how many people seem to think they do not have a root issue. It is true that none of us have "a root issue". We all have many. Often, we have convinced ourselves that we have dealt with everything in our lives as thoroughly and completely as possible. We then insist there is no stressor that has to do with any symptoms. We are so accustomed to stress that there is a tendency to minimize the toll stress is taking.

What is there to be afraid of if there are symptoms and there is no medical explanation?

The symptoms are not necessarily mysterious or unexplainable in nature. They are delivering a very direct and clear message only if we are willing to listen.

Chapter 14 Another Harsh Reality

My peace does not come from controlling my circumstances but from controlling how I manage the complexities of my circumstances.

The big thing about using your voice and walking in this spirit zone is that it may not always accomplish what you thought it would. There is a cost if you allow that to become a reason to stop using your voice. There will always be betrayal, criticism, judgement, and gossip from somewhere at any given time. Though things may seem to go askew, if you are in spirit zone, you stay stable. Why is it important to express what matters to you? Because, what matters to you does matter. It is teaching each person, including yourself, something every time you share it.

Can we begin to consider and realize that each person we meet is teaching us something?

Am I taking leadership of my life?

Children are one of our greatest teachers and our culture is filled with habits that drown out and dismiss the learning opportunities our children bring to the table in all of their innocence.

What are ways we culturally drown out or dismiss what we can learn from children?

Here are a few examples:

- Not valuing their perspective because they are a child.
- Admonishing children for speaking truth that can seem hurtful or rude even when it is spoken from a position of seeking to learn and understand or

simply stating what they see in front of them without the programming of not speaking truth.

- Not teaching descriptive words when they are acting out behaviorally but focusing on the behavior itself.

Improved communication does not mean everyone will agree. We can aim to accomplish respect for each other inside different opinions on a much larger scale than what we have achieved so far.

I learn more from the people who disagree with me than I do from those who agree. With all my heart I want to thank all my patients and every single person that has ever been a part of my life. I've learned so much about people and consequently myself from every encounter in my life.

Generally, here are a few things I've had to accept:

1. My best intentions can be interpreted as harmful/hurtful.
2. No matter how much I tell someone it is safe to tell me anything they need to say to me, if they have not experienced that it is safe (from other experiences unknown to me), it will not happen until something shifts inside *them*.

3. People often will say what they think you want to hear in order to not take the risk of hurting your feelings.
4. People will participate in behaviors that hurt people terribly such as gossip, avoidance, rejection, assert themselves around issues that are not matters of the heart (like a person with an eating disorder insisting they will not eat another bite) and yet they are unable to tell a family member how much they feel controlled by their beliefs which differ from their own.

It gets very complicated because for anyone under the age of 18 who is in a family that insists on certain rigid habits or beliefs, the minor has no choice but to roll with what parents insist on until they can leave and support themselves. Defense mechanisms and habits/patterns have been created for that child (remember, we have all been children) that do not build confidence or satisfying relationship skills in these scenarios. Far too often, the help that is sought (if any) from these types of family systems is a help from inside that system of belief hence further perpetuating the cycle.

Consider the adult man or woman who remains entrenched in symptoms such as eating disorders, anger, panic, substance abuse, depression, anxiety, and especially if the action required involves possibly leaving a relationship(s) or going through the repeated confrontation that must be addressed to bring the relationship(s) into a more satisfying space for each person. Can we also consider that if a relationship does not feel good to you, the other person is likely also not content? This introduces the other complicated variable that people can become so entrenched in the ego zone way of functioning that, from their perspective, any other way of functioning can be extremely threatening (which is part of the conditioning). In this regard, people can find a certain contentment for themselves inside ego zone regardless of how it affects those around them.

Communication can be more than messy. I've certainly had thoughts, feelings, beliefs that through conversations and time to ponder have been shifted into different spaces. The learning should never stop. The conversations should never stop. We cannot control another person or force them to believe what we think we want them to believe. However, the conversations can lead us into a deeper understanding of ourselves, our needs, and just what lengths we are willing to go to for inner peace.

Of what lengths am I speaking?

Are we willing to take absolute responsibility for where we are in our lives?

If I have resentment in my life, it is not because of what that person did to me and I'm, therefore, entitled to resentment. Resentment is a choice that keeps me chained to that experience and every experience I had prior to that experience which resembles the feeling in any way. The person that stirred that resentment in me is showing me where I'm still shackled and that I must take full responsibility for freeing myself from such anguish and suffering. This is the anguish and suffering that filters into all aspects of our lives (the projections) because we accept that as "normal" or we identify it as purely genetic. We treat it like an illness instead of with a greater sense of control or responsibility.

So what must be integrated and practiced to do everything you can inside yourself to decrease undesired symptoms?

What is the true practice?

Consider honesty, being direct, being straightforward, no name calling, no accusations, and not punishment through emotional withdrawal or lashing out emotionally.

Chapter 15 For Children—The Formative Years

To the children, my advice is to not let adults convince you that what you are perceiving is wrong. Adults are often scared and hiding things about themselves as an effort to protect children from adult things. Adults do not like to admit their faults, especially to a child. Many adults persist in defensive attitudes. Many adults are too busy fighting inside (insecure) with how to manage themselves. Most often adults would never admit this to a child because of conditioning in our culture to cater to some belief that children need to be protected from adult issues even though children are drowning in it as it is occurring in their very presence. *How do we continue to make sense of this?* Children need to be taught very early how to deal with the issues they face from any age person from any standpoint.

When you are raised by parents/adults who lie, deceive, avoid reality, avoid conflict, never settle conflicts, and tolerate the intolerable, you are the only one who can determine not to allow yourself to fall into this pit. This is the mission: stay out of the pit. Until the age of 18 when you can make your own decisions, you can certainly be in situations that are beyond stifling. You do not have to let it take you years to recover. Ask yourself if there really has to be a recovery. Once you have that liberty to make your own choices, run and run like wild with the wisdom of your spirit and not with the pain of having been stymied and strained for so many years as that only perpetuates the cycle of separation from your spirit zone.

How is it that parents separate children from their spirit zone?

Everyone is separated from the spirit zone by people telling them who they are, how they are to act, think, feel, and behave. Of course, there must be structure and routine for efficient growth and accountability. There must be the ability to communicate and the ability to actively listen to who this little person is and what you are doing so you can foster that. You must be teaching this little person about their own ego/mind/emotions and how to master that. You must be teaching this little one about projections from others and about our connections with each other. What has really been taught, if a behavior has been forced? Forced "respectful" actions of saying "ma'am and sir" or referring to an adult as Mr. or Mrs. or apologizing when only doing so because was told to may mimic spirit zone but nothing more than conditioning that often creates resentment and lack of respect inside a child. Children are quite capable of reading between the lines. If they go repeatedly without any validation of what they are experiencing, suddenly they too are entrenched in the delusion adults are often creating as they run and hide from themselves.

How can an adult who has never been taught about his own ego/emotions and the concept of cooperation with spirit teach a child?

They cannot. The cycle continues. This results in further separation from spirit zone with efforts from some to connect with spirit zone through the mind on their own accord.

Scenario:

- 11-year-old boy, being raised in a Christian home, 2 younger brothers, and attending a Christian school.
- Experiencing progressive symptoms of anxiety manifesting as nervousness, fearfulness, anger, agitation, irrational fears of not wanting to sleep in own bedroom, tendencies to obsess/dwell
- Open discussion and conversation with this 11-year-old boy indicates high intelligence, independent thinking, and curiosity.
- Questions that challenge the structure in which he is being taught to think are judged as "rebellious" seeming to lead to the feelings of anxiety, sleep problems, agitation, anger, fears.
- The 11-year-old boy has individual ideas and concepts that are not within the norms of his mini–culture hence magnifying his feelings of anxiety.
- The 11-year-old boy has individual ideas of what feels like "play" to him versus his peers. For

example, this boy enjoys landscaping, machinery, developing ideas for decks and walkways. This boy enjoys intellectually stimulating conversations rather than participating in sports.

- Relief of the anxiety (which easily met diagnostic criteria) was resolved with restructuring parenting techniques that allowed individual ideas and placing the child in home schooling for educational structure to develop his gifts and skills rather than squelching his gifts and skills.

- This child no longer has anxiety that is interfering with his level of functioning. Anxiety will always be a red flag for him as to whether he is honoring his own gifts and ideas.

Families, if you have a child with symptoms, I invite you to consider how this child may be a barometer of where there needs to be improved balance in family functioning especially with regards to respect of individual perceptions and attitudes. Children must be included in family discussions when it pertains to the family functioning. Each family member can discuss symptoms created in each person in the family as a direct response of the family functioning. This type of family interaction teaches individuals how to function in this world. Realistically children do know what is going on around them. And, they do not stop thinking about what is going on around them just because they are told to.

Chapter 16 The Ways We Hide

Dear Spirit Zone, forgive me as I buried you so long ago. As I unknowingly pushed you aside in my desperation, I now step back into you to receive your wisdom.

Let's look at this logically:

1. People stay in relationships they do not want to be in so they will not hurt the other person's feelings, because it is easier financially, or because they do not want to be alone.

2. People say yes when they mean no.

3. People defend themselves like they are children well into their adult life if not their entire life.

4. People agree to agree rather than telling the truth of what they really think/feel. Why? Because others might get mad, hurt, or upset.

5. People get lost in the symptoms of their experience rather than removing themselves from the experience regardless of the "risk" (not safety risk) involved. For example: Loss of sleep......seek treatment for sleep loss rather than "fixing" whatever it is that is going on that leads to the sleep loss. Many times there is such a separation from "the stressors" because it is the norm that there is really no awareness of any stressor that could be leading to this symptom.

6. Accusations toward those who do speak out:
   a. Children: rebellious, "talking back", disrespectful
   b. Women: Bitch
   c. Men: Asshole
   d. Those with Mental Illness: Your medication is not working

7. In Roles: "I'm the _____ so I know"

8. In activities: staying busy so as not to have to address issues that need to be addressed

9. In frustration: Attempt after attempt to accomplish or resolve something fails repeatedly, hence leading to a response of tolerance, indifference, frustration or not recognizing there is harshness in the air because it is the "norm". For example: Acceptance of gossip as a real solution or deciding efforts to communicate are fruitless.

10. The roles we play are as follows:

i. Child
ii. Son
iii. Daughter
iv. Friend
v. Father
vi. Mother
vii. Grandmother
viii. Grandfather
ix. Aunt
x. Uncle
xi. Brother
xii. Sister
xiii. Cousin
xiv. Worker

Roles: How they help us, how they hurt us

Help
- Structure
- Routine
- Expectation
- "Societal norms"

Hurt
- Can be limiting
- The role expectation may not align with actual spiritual role
- Role expectation may not fit within societal norms (the way different cultures are perceived, sexual preferences, handicaps)

Consider not giving so much credence to the expectations inside these roles. Consider how these roles put you at risk of falling into magical ideas from role expectations. Where it really matters, in the spirit and soul of our being, these roles serve no purpose other than to give you the opportunity to grow closer to the spirit zone within you or to step yet further away. Take a moment now to contemplate how role conditioning can serve to pull you away from spirit zone.

What if everyone stopped trying to play a part of a role and the societal conditioning that comes with that role and simply operated from their spirit zone?

Every person, every experience, every role gives us this chance over and over and over. The roles inside this life can perpetuate undesired cycles if you use the role expectation as an excuse to stay in a circumstance that is harmful. For example, families are most vulnerable to staying in toxic relationships with each other because of an "obligation" that is conditioned culturally "because it's family". When there is a relationship where one or the other refuses to take responsibility for choices that are hurtful in the relationship, it is conditioning rather than spirit zone that obligates a person to tolerate mistreatment. Allow yourself to consider the idea that this human body is a "suit" for this "force field" (spirit zone) that comes from "a source". In this regard, it is pertinent to operate your "suit" according to the "force" (spirit zone) that is within you rather than inside a magical idea of the conditioning of the role expectation. If not, symptoms will naturally arise in numerous ways.

To reiterate a few of the possible symptoms of such internal discord ("suit" not cooperating with "force field"/spirit zone) consider symptoms such as depression, anxiety, poor sleep, irritability/rage/anger, uneasiness, and insecurity. The diligence put forth to solve these feelings more often by measures outside yourself (either activities/distractions or ego/mind/emotion zone) rather than looking inward to spirit zone far too often is limiting. The proposed limitation is in the concept that the deepest satisfaction is with alignment of ego/emotion/mind to spirit zone (force field). The ideas and activities generated from this alignment bring about the greatest contentment. This is not to say that tools outside you are not useful; but allow spirit zone to direct you to which of those tools you are to use. *How often have you pursued an activity certain it would bring happiness? How often has that sense of satisfaction been only temporary? Or, the activity simply was not satisfying as you had hoped? If you ask yourself now, was I aligned with my spirit zone, what would your answer be?* Following spirit zone is mystical in nature and not always perfectly logical. Hence, the logical reason of the mind and ego can successfully talk you out of listening to this essential part of yourself. Consider that your "mission" on this earth is to sustain alignment with spirit zone first which will then take you into the contentment and satisfaction of whatever goals you are compelled to accomplish.

What is the mission? To remember who we are.

Remember this existence is for a season and you have a mission while you are here. What do you see as spirit zone traits? Love? Joy? Peace? Patience? Kindness? Goodness? Faithfulness? Gentleness? self–control? What traits would you remove from this list or add to this list? Have you bought into the delusion that performing in this existence with these traits is "weakness" or "giving in" in some fashion? Have you ever experienced the power of the ripple effect of these stated traits?

It seems no matter what you do, if you are not aligned with spirit zone; then deep contentment is simply not possible. It is because of the conditioning that starts at birth that you get so tangled in the emotion and ego of the human experiences. It is the roles you occupy that make it seem impossible to function in the spirit zone of your existence.

Participating in defensiveness and blaming your experiences for your unrest will only serve to keep you stuck in the consequence of the experiences and perpetuate separation from your spirit zone. *(Remember, your spirit zone does not need therapy)*. Experiences do separate you from the truth of who you are unless you consciously choose to create a different path for yourself. It is not just the experience that hurt you. It is the separation from the truth of who you really are that perpetuates the emotional pain.

What are some of the defensive responses?

- Confusing spirit concepts with religious beliefs. Following religious truths from the position of ego zone does not equal following spirit zone.
- **Allowing the illusions and logic inside the ego to cloud the whispers from spirit zone.**
- Then the emotions... let us acknowledge now that adults, both male and female alike, have trouble knowing how to deal with the emotional aspect of the human experience. Again, finding the balance

between silence versus explosion and avoiding emotional decision making.

Imagine again but on the other side: no brain, no emotion, no ego but only spirit. Therefore, confident as ever that it is impossible for anything to rob the spirit experience. It is unimaginable that something as simple as emotion and ego could be so powerful, so successfully deceptive. Yet, upon arrival to this suit, ego quickly steps in as the truth, the power, the defense, and the only way to survive. Ego quickly convinces you that listening to spirit zone will only get you further hurt and walked all over.

As I write, my efforts are to reach your spirit zone. My words will easily engage your ego and your mind and perhaps create confusion and arguments against the concepts. This is not an intellectual pursuit. It is a mystical pursuit of listening to your spirit zone and placing your own ego/emotion/mind in alignment with your spirit zone. The only way to be convinced that this is valid is through personal experimentation. The problem with personal experimentation is that the experimenter must allow disciplined intention over time. Conditioning does not change easy, so be cautious to not prematurely decide that following this spirit thing is senseless.

So, how do you truly get a real taste of what it is like to walk in spirit zone? No. It is not about escaping reality and going to a retreat or monastery or nunnery or something of that nature. Perhaps it is like training for a marathon. You must be committed to giving yourself the time it takes to develop the skill, the awareness, the strength, and the shift into following spirit zone as the new default setting.

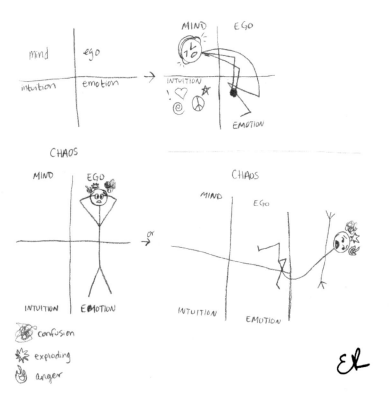

Figure 16-1

Currently, it is likely safe to say that default setting is ego, mind, and emotion as this is our societal norm. There has been so much conditioning from parents, teachers, coaches, experiences, and relationships of all kinds. It is absolutely not about blaming anything on any of the people/experiences that conditioned you as this will only keep you in the loop of staying separated from your spirit zone.

Many people have been convinced that ego and aggressive expression is confidence. So, when spirit zone requests action that is not aggressive or has a different way of "taking up for the self"; too often there is an immediate resistance to taking that course of action. Ego/mind/emotion without spirit zone direction can lead to unreliable outcomes. You must be patient with yourself and persistent in this endeavor of engaging your spirit zone by being completely honest with yourself as to which zone you were in while managing a situation that did not have the outcomes you desired. Ask yourself. *Is it possible that some undesired outcomes in the moment are helping you in some way?* This is where it gets tricky. Our ego does not like undesired outcomes and will quickly take you down a path that can lead to more discouragement if not even despair. *What does your spirit zone say? What happens if*

you stop "fighting" inside yourself and take on the wisdom
from your spirit zone? Do you remember ever not
"fighting" inside yourself?

Is it possible that we get so used to our ego/emotions/mind that we cannot hear spirit? Yes. Unfortunately, therein lies the challenge. Two people trapped in ego cannot lead another person to recognize the spirit zone. Those in caretaking professions may or may not be mastering this process inside themselves and those who you might least expect may be very well acquainted with their spirit zone. Either way, when you want this alignment to spirit zone, everyone and everything around you become your teacher.

Which leads to the next concept. *Can you accept again that everyone and everything is teaching you something? Do not mistake this with falling into analyzing everything as that is simply intellectualization which is another defense mechanism. But, are you seeing patterns in your life? Is there a common theme that always shows up such as anger, insecurity, jealousy, envy? Are there recurrences of poor communication, blame, accusations? Does the same type of scenario keep happening?*

Therein lies the lesson. The opportunity for alignment. Stop escaping, running, avoiding, or making excuses for bad behavior from others but also do not fall into judgement, blame, or criticism which again will only boomerang back to you. Stop allowing yourself to be demeaned by others or your experiences into emptiness or nothingness. You are powerful, amazing, and full of life with passion and a lot to accomplish. Only you have the power to not allow any experience in this world to diminish you into thinking poorly of yourself or being paralyzed about your purpose/mission. That is the very mission while we are here. To not give emotion or ego the leadership in your life but to follow that spirit zone inside you.

> *"**Human beings** have always employed an enormous amount of clever devices for running away from themselves... We can keep ourselves busy, fill our lives with so many diversions, stuff our heads with so much knowledge, involve ourselves with so many people and cover so much ground that we never have time to probe the fearful and wonderful world within... By middle life, most of us are accomplished fugitives from ourselves"* – John Gardner

Chapter 17 Teachers

Forgive me, fellow existence of life, for my judgement and harshness as I lost sight of what you are showing me. You are a gift in my life as I choose to learn from all that you provoke in me.

I've had so many mentors and teachers in my life. Remember ALL encounters no matter how long or brief, direct or indirect, are an opportunity to learn and grow and/or to release something inside that interferes with peace.

I know the fear and pain of letting go of the ways we have been conditioned to believe are the "right" ways of doing things. And better still, I've experienced and witnessed others experiencing the beauty of finally letting go of all that fear and pain while learning to ride life in a different type of security. This is a security that does not come from anything outside yourself but from the confidence within you. This confidence is steadily raped from you from the day of your initial human existence until you realize it is in your control as to whether that form of rape continues.

Rape is a very strong word. Typically, when the word is used, it is in the context of sexual assault. For the context of this discussion, I'm inviting you to consider this possible definition as pulled from www.vocabularly.com/dictionary.

"Rape can also mean to plunder or strip something of resources."

What rapes confidence? All experiences have that capability.

How successful an experience is at raping you from your confidence is based upon which zone you manage the experience. Again, spirit zone will keep you steady and grounded or ego zone will continue to chip away at you until it seems there is no confidence. Because of all the societal conditioning, you are more inclined to fall into ego zone as a default response. Even when you have the awareness and practice of spirit zone, conscious decision making is still required. What this means is that walking in spirit zone is a constant decision by decision choice.

When you respond to experiences from ego zone only, confidence is then disguised in accomplishments, illusions of power such as shaming and guilting others or holding resentment toward others.

Though it can feel good to accomplish certain goals, that satisfaction does not last when the accomplishment is actually a distraction from your separation from spirit zone and entrenchment in the deeper struggles we spoke of earlier.

So, imagine that you came here with a light force (spirit zone) that represents your confidence, strength, peace, clarity, love, compassion and so forth. However, experiences in this world shadow it, bury it, or create a haze over that light source. Everything convinces you that you do not have that light and that you need something else outside yourself more. Perhaps the imagery of light source does not click with you.

What imagery would your spirit zone use?

The name of my private practice came from a conversation I had with a monk in Germany in 1992 around the age of 23. After I had reflected to him that I missed my boyfriend and felt homesick, he said to me "Sometimes it takes the sun a long time to melt the ice so things can come to the surface". In the moment, his statement really did not make sense to me but it stuck with me. Little did I know that I was about to dive into a very deep and important part of my own journey. Initially, I determined that "Melt The Ice" meant uncovering the painful experiences that had been buried and were covertly weighing me down. Now, I see "Melt The Ice", through an additional lens, as more complex than learning how to expose the experiences that have been harmful, painful, troublesome, and burdensome. "Melt The Ice" means finding that pureness deep inside ourselves that knows how to love, that knows confidence, and that simply knows what is needed in any given moment only for that moment. "Melt the Ice" means not just exposing and processing the experiences but letting them melt away.

How might statements like "but my experiences have made me what I'm today" be helpful or harmful?

How can that "making me what I'm today" differ if managed from spirit zone versus ego zone?

Are you afraid of letting your experiences melt away? What part of you is it that is afraid?

Are you supposed to hold on to the experience or the lesson learned?

From what part of yourself are you to identify the lesson learned?

Remember, from the moment you get here you are taught to lose sight of that aspect of yourself because of the way we are trained, conditioned, and programmed. Then you get tangled in a web of symptoms that, if managed from ego zone, will only make the web more complex.

When you focus only on the symptoms, you are falling further away from yourself.

At this stage of my awareness, "Melt The Ice" means discovering the authenticity of who you are and taking each day and each experience with a new perspective. No one has the answers for you. The answers are deep inside you. (This was spoken so beautifully to me by an elder Greek orthodox priest who was my neighbor many years ago)

Chapter 18 Cleaning Your Field and Choosing Your Zone

Dear Spirit Zone, your wisdom awaits my curiosity. Your energy awaits my action. Your reminders of your presence never cease.

Main Points to consider:

1. Trigger vs. actual violation and differences in how to manage

2. Managing a current violation from spirit zone rather than from inside the trigger

3. Clearing all things triggered to gain clarity

HOW TO USE "TRIGGERS":

- Typically, when we get triggered, we want the other person to stop what they are doing so we will not feel triggered.
- More often than not, people get caught in this loop.
- Triggered emotions/memories managed from ego zone equals a vicious cycle. Triggered emotions/memories managed from spirit zone equals progress, growth, and strength.
- When we hold on to past experiences (as is the case inside our culture), we become vulnerable to being triggered and then getting tangled inside a loop of projections. We are vulnerable as long as we hold onto anything that has anything to do with the past. We are only capable of being most clear when we have successfully separated ourselves from our past **(the purpose of meditation practice).**

THE SEPARATION FROM THE PAST:

- Typically, we try to do this through our mind.
- That does NOT always work.

- The separation from the past will be successful for many with disciplined meditation practice. Learning to separate oneself from the ego/mind/emotion by cleansing the Energy Field (which will in turn settle the mind, ego, and emotion in relation to the experience) through imagery/meditation.

FROM THIS ANGLE:

- Meditation may not be such a "feel good" practice at first.

- And until Energy Fields are cleansed; meditation can actually produce more agitation.
  - Here's how:
    - You do a meditation; you remember experiences of countless disrespect (painful to remember) but you successfully find imagery in the meditation that symbolizes the dissolve or release of the impact of the countless experiences where disrespect was present. Now that you have more clarity, you realize you are living in less disrespect, but disrespect, nonetheless. Suddenly, any disrespect feels more agitating,

so this now must be addressed.
Ideally, the release of the experience
is being addressed from a higher
state of awareness rather than as a
"fight".

- THIS IS WHERE BEING TRIGGERED IS
  A "FAVOR" … WE ARE BEING SHOWN
  THAT THERE ARE EXPERIENCES
  TRAPPED IN OUR ENERGY FIELD
  THAT ARE THEN CLOUDING OUR
  PERCEPTION OF OUR CURRENT
  EXPERIENCE.
- THE GOAL IS LEARNING HOW TO
  DISCERN MORE DEEPLY FROM SPIRIT
  ZONE RATHER THAN CIRCULATING
  THROUGH THE PATTERNS AND
  VISCIOUS CYCLES EGO AND
  EMOTION CREATE AROUND OUR
  EXPERIENCES.

Nothing inside us should feel right until we are
aligned with the spirit zone that is packaged inside us. The
very spirit that gives us movement/life/breath. Call it what
you want because getting hung up on words is from the

ego. Regardless, embrace yourself, your visions, and your dreams. The world and those around you may dismiss the possibility of your visions being possible to make a reality; but the truth is that the connection with your spirit zone is a bottomless supply of everything you need to fulfill your mission. You cannot tap into that bottomless supply if you are not attached to your spirit zone. If you are partially aligned without further momentum to improve and sustain the alignment, then you are only limiting yourself. Your mind and ego along with cultural conditioning are the culprits that create the ceilings on what is possible. You have the power and the choice to buy into it or not.

Figure 18-1

Figure 18-2

Chapter 19 Meditation

My mind and my ego have distracted me; but I will hunt you fervently only to discover no hunt was required.

Just like many things, meditation also is taught from many different means of practice. A typical response from those who have attempted meditation or have not had any exposure at all is this idea that meditation was impossible because it was impossible to quiet the mind.

On that note, I say that it is indeed impossible to quiet the mind, especially if that is the zone you are occupying.

So, release any idea that meditation is supposed to be *instantly* calming, relaxing, and soothing. Give yourself time with learning to meditate when that is not accomplished rapidly. The practice is often given up on far too soon.

Consider that meditation is not just about what is happening in the time that you are meditating. Meditation is about creating desired changes in your life. How? If you cannot get past your mind in your meditation, then is your meditation practice not showing you where you are? Can this awaken you to how much you are using your mind without spirit zone consultation in your daily decisions. It is not the meditation that is a way of life. Meditation is a tool to clear your access to your spirit zone. The "way of life" part is living in alignment with spirit zone.

Do your efforts to meditate show you what is blocking that?

Do your meditation efforts show you fleeting thoughts or ideas of how to shift that block?

Spirit zone creates a lot of action... it is not a lazy zone.

What type of action might spirit zone be suggesting to you?

Are you acquainted with the nature of spirit zone?

Remember spirit zone brings no harm, no negativity. Spirit zone is not a pushover but knows how to confront life with compassion and grace.

Do you think this means you will not have emotion?
Is it possible that the spirit zone force could be prompting you so clearly that the force of that compelling creates an anxiety of sorts?

Are you afraid of that power inside you?

Do you know how to work with that power inside you?

There is serious disappointment when the expectation of meditation is to experience some sort of bliss. That is the long–term outcome if your meditation leads you to alignment with spirit zone. Meditation is your consultation time with spirit zone. Allow time for yourself to learn to occupy spirit zone without mind zone interference. Initially meditation takes commitment, perseverance, and determination as you sit to see what it is inside yourself. Allow the experiences/memories/emotions that remain deeply embedded to replay rather than avoiding these experiences/memories/emotions. BUT then use the meditation practice as a means of releasing and cleansing oneself from the undesired impact and patterns created from the experiences rather than dwelling, over processing, or avoiding. Yes, that is correct.... sitting in silence is going to allow every experience you prefer to never remember again to surface. So, I emphatically state you also have to know how to use the meditation to dissolve these experiences rather than reliving it in such a way that it robs and destroys your peace.

This takes practice as it seems that it is our human nature to do everything possible to forget unpleasant experiences rather than learning to shed the experience from your current existence. Yes, it is possible to shed the intensity of the emotion created from the experience and the consequent ripple effect of the patterns inadvertently created by the experience. Cleansing is accomplished by using meditation as a method to reclaim your Energy Field and consult with your spirit zone. Then even though the memory may recur on occasion, the downward spiral that can ensue is interrupted.

What I've learned through my experience of Bodhi Yuj is that if I do not put forth effort to cleanse and reclaim my Energy Field; it is impossible to gain control of the mind or emotions as those zones will quickly fall into past experiences and rehash everything over and over. I've witnessed inside my own life and the lives of many others the frustrations and dissatisfaction of working hard to try to create a cognitive shift or an emotional shift without any attention to the Energy Field. I certainly witnessed dissatisfaction with simply trying to pray something away. An uncleansed Energy Field will keep the mind and emotions and ego operating full tilt. Whereas, using spirit zone wisdom to cleanse the Energy Field is a process that can settle the mind and emotions. Keeping the ego at bay is a constant decision by decision process by asking oneself "Which zone am I occupying?"

The Ego?
The Spirit?
The Mind?
The Emotions?

How is my meditation helping me be aligned with my spirit zone moment by moment?

Chapter 20 My Journey

What an enchanting process.

I finally decided to go meet Achito and visit his store in 2015. In my head, I was not visiting for myself as much as I was visiting to inquire about his willingness to do a meditation class for patients at the clinic where I worked. Achito proposed that perhaps I should attend a meditation class to see his style, first-hand, before taking any further steps. The location of his meditation class along with the time of day really did not work with my schedule. I simply did not want to surround myself with more people as one of my favorite ways to recharge has always been through some sort of outdoor activity. The solution was for me to have privately scheduled appointments with him.

First, I would like to share that since 1999, I became aware of myself in a more interesting way. I started to recognize that I had a sensitivity of sorts. I would describe it as a heightened awareness or a strong intuition. The problem I encountered over and over is that most people I encountered (except for my patients) did not want to acknowledge the realities of these unspoken undercurrents. So, despite the benefits of having this heightened awareness, it came with hardships. These hardships came in the form of being confused about what work I still needed to do versus clarifying within myself that I was only picking up on what someone else was experiencing.

Achito's teachings about the practice of Bodhi Yuj changed my experience of this transference. I now have clarity as to what is mine and what is information coming to me even if unspoken. I have a greater appreciation for the ripple effects of what I exude both intentionally and unintentionally. By embracing these concepts and exploring the validity in my own life, I experience more clarity in managing the unavoidable emotional content we must all navigate in our human form. Each day, each moment, I recognize my choice to truly live in the power of today. The choice of removing the contamination of the past, the projections of others, and to not allow the past experiences projected by others to incidentally rob my present situation. I have witnessed that the more I free myself, the more I see many of those in contact with me also finding freedom. The miracles continually unfold.

Having read a lot of materials that proved very rich and meaningful in my life; it was not until bringing this practice into my life that everything seemed to come alive. This practice showed me how to appreciate what the mind, emotion, ego, and past bring to the table; yet no longer having to work so hard to manage it. On the same token, this practice is a daily practice. It is a daily commitment. It is a way of life. It's not about intellectually learning about it, participating in a seminar for a day and having some lightbulb come on, or about integrating it sporadically. Just like many things, you get out of it what you put into it. The practice is not a miracle cure, nor does it prevent hardships or challenges. The primary beautiful aspect of this practice is that it enhances *you*. This practice is not confining, restrictive, or rigid. The practice can be integrated into any religious beliefs you bring to the table as it is a process of removing the barriers inside your own life that keep you trapped in undesired patterns established from experiences.

Can you imagine living without your past experiences contaminating your life today?

Can you imagine having the clarity and confidence necessary to manage the situations that show up in your life?

For professionals in caretaking positions: this practice can broaden and empower the therapeutic opportunities in your patient interactions. It can amplify the meaning of transference and countertransference into very powerful tools to further one's own healing as well as the healing of the one you sit with.

For all others: this practice and these concepts have the potential to help you find a strength inside yourself long forgotten and to find a sincere appreciation for all encounters as an opportunity that takes you deeper into your own wisdom, clarity, and strength while consequently providing the same opportunity for all those around you as your undercurrent shifts to one of compassion, love, integrity, and strength.

Only serious readers who are committed to the journey will have the chance to find this as a transformative way of life; not a miracle cure/answer.

In my professional role, I aim to help the seeker find that intricate balance in the necessary tools to maintain our grounding in a world where change is constant. I aim to help you find that balance in creating and accomplishing your desired path. Does it include medication, counseling, coaching, skills training, community involvement, spiritual development, or any other multitude of tools necessary to confidently navigate your experiences? These are the explorations that help bring clarity into your process. It takes time and commitment with full appreciation of the complexities of our human existence.

Afterward

Throughout the years as I met with patients, I would often hear them say "you should write a book". Typically, I would smile and think "no way". After a while, I started to hear that prompting enough that I thought I should take it more seriously. I have certainly never identified myself as an author, nor do I plan to write more books. If I were to narrow it all down to a sentence I would say, "Stay away from defensiveness and learn to trust your intuition".

When people ask me what to read when I begin the process of teaching the principles introduced in this book; I find it challenging to know where to point that individual. Mostly because there are thousands of books, articles, websites, documentaries, and literature that reflect these concepts from many different angles. I wrote this book as a starting point for the people I meet with and encourage all readers to continue your exploration. It has been my experience that it is important to give thoughtful consideration to many concepts as our human complexities do not fit a "one size fits all" mentality.

I want to express gratitude for the scientific advances that give us more and more alternatives for those who do suffer with mental illness that benefit from the assistance of psychotropic medications. Sometimes the body simply needs that assistance so principles discussed, and skills learned can be successfully applied. My utmost respect goes out to all of who suffer with mental illness as you personally seek that balance inside yourself as to what you can expect from medication versus what must be addressed through the application of other tools as well.

Last, as I completed the first draft of this book; my mother passed. I want to express gratitude to my sisters who mysteriously encouraged me to sit privately with our mother as she passed. The entire unfolding of this sacred transitioning experience goes beyond words. My mother and I were very different women in many ways, yet similar in our sensitivity. I will never forget the words she uttered to me as she was fading in and out of this reality. She said, **"Be well, but not at the expense of others**." To this I would add: Remember, **being powerful** does not mean being aggressive.

About the Author

Marsha grew up in a small town in Virginia. Even though she was always adventurous, she did not start traveling until her undergraduate studies required a cross cultural experience. Since then, she has had the privilege of not only traveling around the United States but also to many other countries. This exposure sharpened her appreciation for "differences" in many shapes and forms. She has always loved being a nurse and then later a nurse practitioner and especially appreciates the opportunity she has now to be in private practice in order to provide treatment in an environment that allows the time necessary for the unexpected things that can show up.

For her leisure and personal life, she is happily married on a small farm in yet another rural town in Virginia. She enjoys hiking, biking, boating, music, social gatherings, salsa dancing, and of course her two horses, two dogs, and her cat.

"Sometimes it takes the Sun a long time to melt the ice so things can come to the surface."

Melt The Ice

Marsha D. Stonehill

Thank you!

13596350R20086